STREETWISE

STREETWISE

PHOTOGRAPHS BY MARY ELLEN MARK

Introduction by John Irving

Text and Photographs edited by Nancy Baker

From the Film *STREETWISE* by
Martin Bell · Mary Ellen Mark · Cheryl McCall

upp

University of Pennsylvania Press

PHILADELPHIA

Typographic design by Carl Gross

The preliminary version of this book was designed by Roger
Gorman, Frances Reinfeld, Reiner Design Consultants, Inc.

Library of Congress Cataloging-in-Publication Data

Mark, Mary Ellen, 1940–
    Streetwise / photographs by Mary Ellen Mark; introduction by
John Irving; text and photographs edited by Nancy Baker.
    p.   cm.
    "From the film Streetwise by Martin Bell, Mary Ellen Mark,
Cheryl McCall."
    ISBN 0-8122-1268-1 (pbk.)
    I. Baker, Nancy, 1946–   II. Bell, Martin, 1943–   Streetwise.
III. Title.
PN1997.S7763M37   1988
791.43′72—dc19   87-30228
                                                CIP

Dedicated to DEWAYNE POMEROY
and LOU ELLEN COUCH

ACKNOWLEDGMENTS

We wish to thank the following people and organizations
for their help with this book: LIFE Magazine, Richard B. Stolley,
John Loengard, Melvin L. Scott, Jerry Esterly, Gary Schneider,
Sidney Rapoport, Kathleen Brennan, Connie Nelson,
Willie Nelson, and Tom Waits.

*Our gratitude to the following people
who shared their lives with us:*

Alabama	Kevin
Annie	Lillie
Antoine	Lora Lee
Baby Gramps	Lulu
Biker Kim	Melissa
Black Junior	Michele
Breezy	Mike
Buddha	Munchkin
Butch	Patrice
Calvin	Patti
Chrissie	Peehole
Dawn	Rat
Dewayne	Red Dog
Drugs	Roberta
Eddie	Russ
Erica	Sam
Floyd	Shadow
J.R.	Shellie
James	Smurf
Jimi	Sparkles
John	Tiny
Juan	Tracy
Justin	White Junior
Kim	William

PREFACE

In April 1983 reporter Cheryl McCall and I traveled to Seattle, Washington, to do an article for LIFE Magazine on runaway children. One of the reasons we chose Seattle was because it is known as "America's most livable city." Los Angeles, San Francisco and New York were well known for their street kids. By choosing America's ideal city we were making the point "If street kids exist in a city like Seattle then they can be found everywhere in America, and we are therefore facing a major social problem of runaways in this country."

Seattle is a beautiful city. We spent our first few days driving around the downtown area looking for places where the kids might hang out.

Cheryl and I had a long working experience together on several difficult stories. We trusted each other's instincts, and were an excellent working team because we totally immersed ourselves in a story and tried to get as close to our subjects as possible. We became obsessed with finding and meeting Seattle street kids.

I will never forget the first time we saw our kids by the graffiti wall between First and Second on Pike Street. We had driven past that wall many times before and it was always empty. That particular day we drove by around four thirty in the afternoon and the wall was transformed into a meeting place for kids. This is where we began our story on Seattle's street children.

At first they were very suspicious of us. They were sure we were undercover cops. We showed the teenagers magazines and books with previous stories that we had done, but nothing would persuade them.

I think that there were two important factors that helped convince the kids that we were o.k. The first was my getting a jaywalking ticket and having an argument with the policeman who gave it to me. The kids gathered around and watched the dispute. They were impressed that I stood up to a cop. The second factor that brought us closer to the kids was Lulu's accepting us.

Lou Ellen Couch was a nineteen-year-old girl from a large and turbulent Seattle family. She had been on and off the street since she was nine years old. She was gay, and at the time we met her she was involved in a difficult relationship with a girl named Wendy. Lulu was by far the most loved and respected person among the street kids. She was high strung and emotional and she had a major drinking problem, but she also had an extraordinary sense of justice.

Lulu was constantly defending the kids she felt had been done wrong. As a result she often fought with men and women much bigger or stronger than herself. She always gave them a good fight and most of the time she won, but as a result of her con-

stant battles she often had a black eye and a scarred and battered look. Sometimes she reminded me of a sad but feisty old alley cat. Lulu was an extraordinary character and Cheryl and I were immediately drawn to her. When Lulu decided that we were o.k. most of the kids accepted us.

One by one we met the group of street kids that we came to know, write about, and photograph. We met a sad and lonely Shadow on his eighteenth birthday and celebrated with him. He in turn introduced us to his friend and "popcorn pimp" competitor Munchkin, who introduced us to his combative girlfriend Patti.

Every Friday and Saturday night the kids would gather at a questionable Seattle discotheque called "The Monastery." Most of the street kids didn't have the entrance fee so they would hang out in the parking lot. They would run from car to car, drink beer or whiskey, buy and sell drugs, and generally get high. The energy and expectancy level in that parking lot was highly charged. Occasionally fist fights would break out and there was a continuous entrance and exit of cars on the lot.

The first time I saw Erin Blackwell was in this parking lot. A big station wagon taxi pulled up and two little girls looking about ten and twelve stepped out. The one who looked twelve was actually almost fourteen and her street name was Tiny. The other was her friend Phillis and she was eleven. They both wore tight sweaters, tight jeans, and lots of make-up. They looked like little girls playing "dress up" and they were amazing. I approached them, introduced myself, and asked if I could spend time with them to take pictures. They both started to giggle and ran towards a waiting car. The next day Teresa, a social worker, introduced Cheryl and me to Tiny. She also assured her that we were journalists not police. That was the beginning of a long relationship which continues today.

One day an old merchant seaman named George approached us on Pike Street. He heard about the story we were doing and he knew two young boys that we just had to meet. The boys were called Rat and Mike and they lived in an abandoned building. He said the younger boy looked like a little kid and was a real character.

The next day George took us to the abandoned building which was several blocks away. We borrowed a ladder and the three of us climbed up into the building.

I was really glad that George was with us, even though he was an old man and I don't know how he would have helped us if we were attacked. It just felt better to have him there. The interior of the building was beyond terrifying. It was dark and deserted and full of garbage and broken glass. There was evidence that people lived there: old mattresses, bottles, rotten food, and even some old *Playboy* magazines. George took us down a long hallway to the room where Rat and Mike lived. We knocked on the door but there was no answer. The entrance to the room seemed to be blocked by a piece of furniture. We found another way into the space through an adjoining room. Once inside we found it was empty but we felt that people lived there and that they would return. There was an old couch in the room, probably moved from another part of the building. There were music and movie posters on the walls and in the corner there was a lace-up pair of roller skates. Cheryl and I left a note for Rat and Mike saying that we would return to find them.

A few days later we came back to the abandoned building. We arrived there this time at six a.m., because we felt it was a sure time to catch the boys still sleeping. George didn't want to come with us that early so Cheryl's friends Rick and Connie followed us to the building in their pick-up. Thinking about entering the building alone made us really nervous, so the understanding was that every ten minutes Cheryl and I would wave from a window in the building to Rick and Connie. This way they would know that all was o.k. and this gave us a sense of security. We found the room and knocked on the door. This time there was clearly someone inside. We pushed the door open and saw four people asleep in the room. Three boys were buried in sleeping bags; one slept on the couch. Two of the boys looked older. They could have been in their late twenties and looked more like hobos. The other two were younger. They introduced themselves as Rat and Mike and they were both sixteen years old. Rat looked more like a twelve-year-old and he was actually the leader of the two. Mike acted as his protector. The two boys were from Sacramento. They had run together after arguing with their families. They lived by begging, stealing, and eating from dumpsters. While searching for food in a dumpster Rat found a pair of roller skates, and he loved to skate up and down the hallways of the abandoned building.

The next morning I spoke to my husband Martin. He is a film-maker and we often talked about working together. I told him about the strange and fascinating lives of the Seattle street children, and I told him about a kid named Rat roller skating down the hallway of an abandoned building. At that moment we all decided that we must come back to Seattle and make a film.

Cheryl and I returned to New York in mid May. In July 1983 our article appeared in LIFE Magazine.

In late August 1983 Cheryl, Martin, and I returned to Seattle to make *Streetwise*. Cheryl raised $80,000 from her friend Willie Nelson. The additional money needed to shoot the film was invested by the three of us. We totally believed in the project because we knew that the kids had a special story to tell.

We found Tiny, Lulu, and Rat still in Seattle; Rat's partner Mike was gone. He was in a juvenile jail in California. Other children were also gone and there were many new kids on the street. In many ways it was like starting all over again.

The first night of shooting Martin did something that proved to be an excellent lesson in gaining access to the kids. We were filming in the Dismas Center, which is a facility open to kids for food, counseling, and recreation. Suddenly Chrissie, a sixteen-year-old street kid, became very angry with Martin for filming her. Martin, to everyone's amazement, opened his camera magazine and gave her the exposed strip of film. Chrissie stormed out the door holding the strip of film which I later found crumpled on the sidewalk. After that incident, whenever we saw Chrissie on the street all that she wanted was to be filmed and to be our friend. When Martin gave the exposed film to Chrissie he showed her and the other kids that we were not trying to steal something from them—if they wanted to be part of the film that was fine but if they didn't want to that was o.k. too. We knew that it was hard for these kids to trust anyone, but we hoped that they would learn to trust us a bit.

When we were shooting on the street, Lulu's accepting us was once again a major factor in helping us gain access to the other kids. One by one we met the main characters in our film.

We were introduced to Dewayne, a fragile sixteen-year-old boy who had been in a juvenile facility while we did our story for LIFE Magazine. His mother had deserted him and his father was in jail. He lived in a trailer with a young street couple and their newborn son. He ran errands for them, and in return they gave him food and a place to sleep. We learned that he was going to visit his father in jail and immediately sought permission to film the visit. This meeting between Dewayne and LeRoy Pomeroy was one of the most moving scenes in the film.

In every successful still photographic project that I have completed there has always been a turning point in the story where I felt that perhaps I was working on something that could be very special. This happened three weeks into our filming in Seattle.

All of us felt that Tiny could be a very strong character in the film. When we first started to work with her we were a bit disappointed because she was too self-conscious. One afternoon we decided to film her while she visited her mother Pat, who worked in a local coffee shop.

When Pat finished work we followed them home to the tiny shack that they shared. Pat started to drink beer and play solitaire and Tiny went into the bedroom. They started to argue, and an intense personal conversation developed between mother and daughter that touched the core of their relationship.

As a still photographer I had photographed many situations that were highly emotionally charged. Even though those situations sometimes led me to take very strong photographs, when I looked at my contact sheets I always remembered the real situation as being even stronger than the photograph. With the filming of Tiny's and Pat's argument, for the first time I was seeing something unfold before me that was being totally captured. That was an extraordinary feeling. We filmed many moving scenes with Tiny and she became a major character in the film. By chance she fell in love with Rat which led to a sad and beautiful departure scene when Rat left Seattle a few weeks later.

We all worked long and hard hours. Cheryl was brilliant at dealing with social service agencies and gaining access to families and institutions. I worked as a link between Cheryl and Martin and tried to help Martin, especially when he was filming on the street. With all of the stress, anxiety, and quick tempers that film-making can bring, none of us ever disagreed about the point of view of the film, it was a film about the kids as told by the kids. It was their story.

One big difference between still photography and film is that film is a collaborative medium that requires several people and much more equipment. When you are shooting intimate scenes it is more difficult in film than in still photography to be a "fly on the wall." Most of the intimate scenes were filmed with just Martin and sound recordist Keith Desmond present, because Martin wanted as little distraction as possible.

When it was time to leave Seattle it was very difficult to say goodbye to the kids. Halloween was our last night of shooting and there was a party at the Dismas Center. All the kids came in costume. Shadow wore a skull mask and a top hat. A thirteen-year-old girl named Lillie came as a mouse with a red nose, whiskers, and a green wig. She gave us each a tulip bulb to plant so we would not forget her. Tiny looked very grown up and beautiful in a hat with a veil, a short black dress, and dark stockings. She told us she was dressed as a French whore.

Sunday, the day before we left Seattle, Martin and I drove to Tiny's house to say a last goodbye. She had been out all night and was still in bed. She looked so sad and vulnerable, so alone. "Take me with you," she said. I told her that if she lived with us she would have to go to school like a normal fourteen-year-old. I also told her that at night she would have to be home at a reasonable hour and that she would not be allowed to hang out on the streets.

"Forget it," she said. "I don't want to go back to school because I would have to go back to the sixth grade where all the kids are only twelve years old. It would be too embarrassing."

She propped herself up on some pillows. She had just gotten a permanent, and she suddenly looked older. "I could never leave the street," she said. I took one last picture of her. She was wearing a T-shirt that had a prominent 16 on it.

We returned to New York and eventually raised additional finances for post-production. When Martin met Nancy Baker he knew she was exactly the right person to edit the film. They spent many months working together in the editing room. Cheryl returned to LIFE Magazine to report and write and I continued my work as a freelance photographer.

In July 1984 Cheryl and I were assigned by LIFE to do a story in Minneapolis on sexually abused children. One afternoon I was photographing a mother with her two daughters in their home when suddenly I had a strong impulse to call home and speak to Martin. I asked if I could use the phone. The line was constantly busy, and when I finally got through Martin told me that he had just been speaking with Jerry Esterly, who had phoned to tell him that Dewayne Pomeroy had hung himself in a juvenile correctional institution the night before his seventeenth birthday. Martin, Cheryl, and I immediately returned to Seattle. Dewayne's death was a great tragedy. He was about to get released from the juvenile facility and we felt that the idea of facing the streets alone again was just too much for him.

In October of 1984 we returned to Seattle to show the completed film to the kids. This was the first public showing in this country of *Streetwise*, and it was for all of us the most terrifying.

If the kids in the film did not like the film or if they felt betrayed by it then we would have failed.

About fifty street kids and a few parents and social workers piled into a small room in a social center in Seattle. During the first part of the film the kids laughed and hollered whenever they saw themselves on the screen. Lulu was especially excited about being in the film. She brought a group of friends with her and all of them roared with laughter whenever Lulu appeared. Halfway through *Streetwise* the mood of the story changes, and the film becomes more serious. At that point, the room became silent. By the end of the film many of the children were in tears. One boy approached Martin. "Are our lives really like this?" he asked. He then continued, "I want to hit someone but I don't know who to hit."

The street children of Seattle embraced the film as their own. They felt it was truly their story. The only criticism that they had was that we were not present at a memorial service for Dewayne Pomeroy they held a week after his death. They planted a tree in his memory in Freeway Park. Teresa from the Dismas Center gave each of them a balloon and told them to think of something that they would like to say to Dewayne. They then released all the balloons over the park. The children thought that it would have been good for us to film this, and they were right.

Postscript

Today Erin Blackwell has two children. She has a boy named Daylon born February 5 1985. I photographed his delivery and it was an unusually easy birth. On May 1 1987 she gave birth to a girl who she named LaShawndrea. The baby was born at ten minutes to three in the afternoon. Two hours and twenty minutes later Jerry Esterly came to visit her. He found her sitting at a table in her room with a cigarette in her mouth playing backgammon with another young patient. When she saw Jerry, she jumped up and said, "Want to see her?" She then trotted down the hallway to show him the baby.

In December 1985 Martin received a call from Lou Ellen Couch's sister. Lulu had been stabbed to death in a street fight while defending a friend. Her last words were, "Tell Martin and Mary Ellen Lulu died."

During the past three years much of the area around the Pike Street Market has been renovated. It is rapidly becoming gentrified. The grafitti wall has not been torn down yet and it is still a gathering place for street kids. Many of the kids that we knew still meet there from time to time and of course there are many new street children. The oldtimers talk about how things have changed and how it will never be the same without DeWayne and Lulu there. Sometimes they will take a new kid across the street to the Pike Street Market and show them two plaques on the ground. Plaque 21393 says "Lulu Couch 1985" and Plaque 21394 says "Dewayne Pomeroy 1984."

Mary Ellen Mark
New York City
July 18, 1987

INTRODUCTION

John Irving

The children of Pike Street are runaways; when I first saw Mary Ellen Mark's photographs of them—in the spring of 1983—I knew they were perfect characters for an important story, because they were both perfect and important victims. The characters in any important story are always victims; even the survivors of an important story are victims. At the time, Seattle's Green River Killer had already murdered 28 young girls, yet the teenagers of Pike Street were holding their own—pimps, prostitutes, and petty thieves, they were eating out of dumpsters, falling in love, getting tattooed, being treated for the variety of venereal diseases passed on to them by their customers.

All teenagers plan for unlikely futures—"three yachts or more"—and lifetime lovers, but the children of Pike Street must conduct their dreaming in the presence of expediencies far darker than most Americans can imagine. Tiny is a fourteen-year-old girl, malnourished, an accomplished prostitute with a lengthy record of occupational diseases; her alcoholic mother says that Tiny's prostitution is "just a phase." Dewayne is a sixteen-year-old boy; he visits his father, a failed arsonist, in prison. Dewayne's father fails as a father, too; Dewayne is one of the victims of Pike Street who won't survive this story.

More than a year after I saw Mary Ellen's pictures of these children, I saw the rough cut of her husband's movie. Martin Bell is an Englishman, which makes the powerful authenticity of his film all the more impressive to me: that he could so thoroughly have gained the trust of Tiny and Dewayne and the others—that he has succeeded in getting them to accept the presence of his camera so unselfconsciously, so completely gracefully. These children's voices are heartbreaking; their tone is mostly deadpan, sometimes dreamy, relentlessly honest. It is the narrative technique of *Streetwise* that makes you forget you're watching a documentary; the absolutely natural quality of the children's voices has the storytelling exactness of fiction. And the unobtrusive quality of the camerawork contributes to the impression that *Streetwise* is as concrete and inevitable as a good novel.

I saw the finished version of Martin Bell's movie not long after President Reagan's landslide victory. I wish the president could see *Streetwise*, for there is little acknowledgment of the existence of Pike Street's children in his plans for America. At a time when so many of the self-righteous are crusading for the rights of the unborn, who is paying attention to the *born?* Mary Ellen Mark and Martin Bell have been paying attention to the children of Pike Street, who are very much born—and unloved, poor, unwanted, abused. Like all good stories, *Streetwise* is timely. I wish that the national (and presidentially approved) fervor for fetuses could be slightly redirected. Dewayne and Tiny and their friends Rat and Shadow and Munchkin—they all managed to be born. But who is taking care of them?

FOREWORD

Jerry Esterly

"I gotta get off the streets, Jerry. Can you help me find my sister? Maybe I can stay with her. She's someplace in California. My Mom's in California or Arizona, I'm not sure. I think my Grandmother in Oregon knows where."

For the past twenty years I have worked as a Juvenile Parole Counselor. I'm working with some kids whose parents I used to have on parole. I've seen a lot of stuff, but nothing like the current street scene.

Every week kids drift into my office. Maybe they used to be on parole or maybe they just saw me around. Many street kids are escaping from homes where they have been abused emotionally, physically, and sexually, or from homes where they have found no love or understanding. Some are searching for excitement and some simply drift there because they have no other place to be or to go. When they first hit the streets they are young, cocky, full of fun, and excited about life. After a few years they are eighteen, nineteen, or twenty and the excitement and fun have gone. The streets wear them down. They do too much, they see too much and have too much responsibility. They can't take the time to learn and grow. Rather than expanding, their world narrows.

The streets are tough and those that have other places to go soon leave. Those that can't, like the kid I'm talking to, have had to scheme, "dumpster dive" for discarded food, panhandle, meter pick, rob, steal, sell dope and their bodies to get by. They get old and desperate, so they come in and we talk.

"If this placement with your sister doesn't come through (they seldom do), how about a program? I can get you into a mission for a day or two. I know it's just temporary, but then maybe something will come up." "Thanks, Jerry. Sounds good. Maybe I'll check that out later and get back to you on that."

The kid says, "How about a job?" A job is a luxury few of these kids can afford because it requires the resources to last the two weeks or a month until the first pay check. I look at this beat-up kid in front of me. Rotten teeth, dirty clothes, no job skills, and little idea of what it takes to get or hold a job. I wonder if he found a job how he could keep it.

So I say "Great idea but I don't have any sure job leads right now. How about a program to help you get a few more job skills? They help find work too, you know."

He looks down. We both know those programs take more time and energy than he is probably able to spend. He says, "Thanks, Jerry, sounds good. I'll get back to you on that one." You see the real reason this kid is in my office is he is sinking and praying someone will save him before he goes under. He needs that miracle, that sister or someone to make it right. He needs food, shelter, clothing, and stability—a place to dream of better things.

In reality these things are probably only going to be available to him in prison. I say probably because once in a while a kid will get lucky. But I wonder if a long shot doesn't come through pretty soon just when this kid will go for the big score, thinking, "If I make it big, great, if not what the hell."

Some are in prison now and at least have food and shelter. Some are dead. They can't be hurt any more. It's funny how we will spend thousands of dollars to lock these kids up and spend nickels and dimes when they're out there on the street and need our help. I wonder most about all those kids who don't seek somebody out. What is the future for the growing numbers that are out there just drifting. I wonder too about the next generation. What kind of parents will these kids be? What kind can they be?

STREETWISE

Tiny on Pike Street

"She has grown up quite a bit since she's been on these streets. She's four-teen going on twenty-one."

TINY'S MOTHER

Pike Street area

"I wasn't even thinking about running away or nothin'. But my dad told me that if I ever got caught selling pot, never come home 'cause he'd kill me. So when it all came down, I just said, 'oh, well'." RAT

Tiny and friends

"For a blow-job it would be $30 on up and for a lay it would be $40 on up. Most of these veterinarian ho's would charge more than us little kids do."

TINY

Laurie and the Ferret Man

Laurie

"I think it is very strange that older men like little girls. They're perverts is what they is." TINY

"So who cares. I don't really care. Whatever happens, happens."   KIM

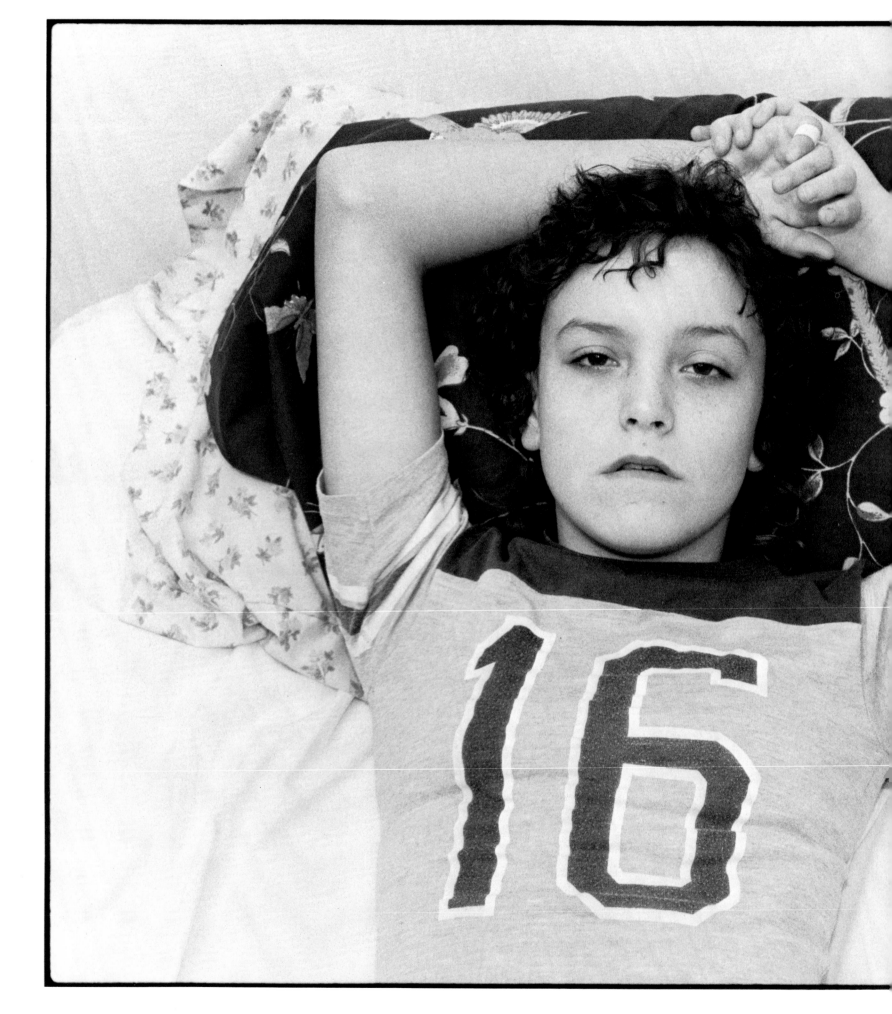

"I wanna be really rich . . .
and live on a farm with a
bunch of horses, which is
my main best animal . . .
and have three yachts or
more . . . and diamonds
and jewels and all that
stuff."

TINY

"When I first met Patti, she was beatin' the heck out of some old dude 'cause he said something wrong to her."

SHADOW

"You learn how to fight or you disappear. I know how to fight but I like disappearing." SHADOW

Lillie

"I don't want to see her get beat up. She's too young."   LULU

Patti and Munchkin

Rat and Mike

"When we'd get real low on money, I'd take Mike's .45, because I'd sold my .38, and I'd go roll a queer."

RAT

"There's this abandoned hotel . . ."

". . . And we'd carry water up in these gallon jugs, 'cause it didn't have no water or electricity. It was pretty easy actually."   RAT

"When you get regular dumpsters, we call 'em regs, you go there every night."   RAT

"Sir, you wouldn't be able to help me out with a little change, would you?"

"No." "Not at all, huh? Ya know, you're a fuckin' dick."   RAT

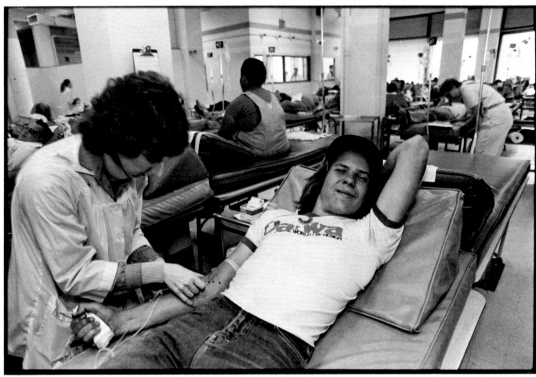

"If you get a fake ID, then you can go there and sell blood."   JAMES

"You're like me, Dewayne,
you're a con man. A smart-
ass little punk."

DEWAYNE'S FATHER

"We don't mean to scare you, we're just telling you the truth. You get beat up, some of these girls end up getting killed."

"My fear is that someday I'm going to get a phone call or a knock at my door and she's not going to be there any more."   PAT, TINY'S MOTHER

"She thought I would be really angry with her and hate her, but I don't. It's just a phase she's going through right now. I can't stop her from doing this. She's just going to do it anyway."   PAT, TINY'S MOTHER

"Every person, no matter how big or tough they are, should always have a partner."

RAT

"I considered myself dependent upon a couple of girls supporting me, but as far as being a pimp, I never pushed them out onto the streets. A playboy is what I consider myself."   SHADOW

"I've thought about not being a lesbian, but then every guy I've ever been with has screwed me over anyway
. . . To tell you the truth, I've got to like somebody alot to even kiss 'em."   LULU

Dawn and Lulu

"Let me get your phone number so I can call you so we can go out for pizza or somethin'." DEWAYNE
"I don't have a phone right now." KIM

"Patti and Munchkin . . . were, in my eyes, made for each other." SHADOW

"They argue, but doesn't all love affairs argue?"   SHADOW

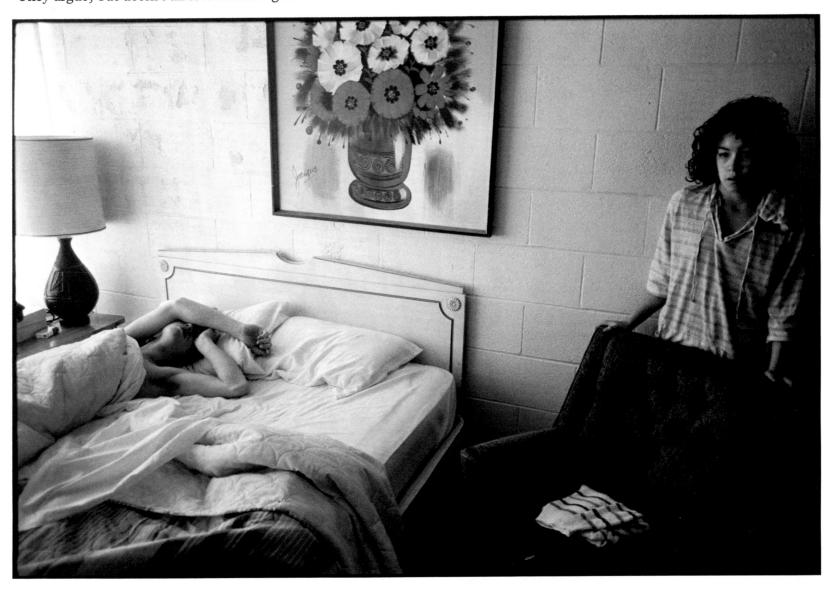

"I think she likes Tom. She just doesn't want to admit it."   PAT, TINY'S MOTHER

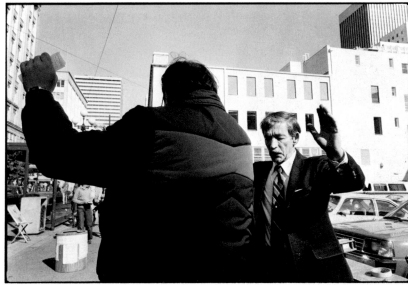

"If you want joy, you must jump for it."
REVEREND TOM ROBINSON

"Why do you want to dye your hair? To change?" "Not to change. To get away from everything."   SHADOW

"We got in a fight. She was drunk that night. The next day she felt really bad." TINY

"The reason why I think Rat is cute and the reason why I love him so much is because he's got pretty eyes. I think they're brown or blue, one or the other."   TINY

"She just wants to get too serious at too young of an age. She's only fourteen years old and she makes it sound like she's ready to get married."   RAT

"I want a baby. But not by a new trick though."   TINY

"I love to fly . . . The only bad part about flying is having to come back down to the fuckin' world."   RAT

Tiny, "Don't leave." Rat, "I got to." Tiny, "Then take me with you."

"Get a girl friend, have a house or a car or somethin', have a little money in the bank. Get a job. That's what I expect out of life. Not much."   DEWAYNE

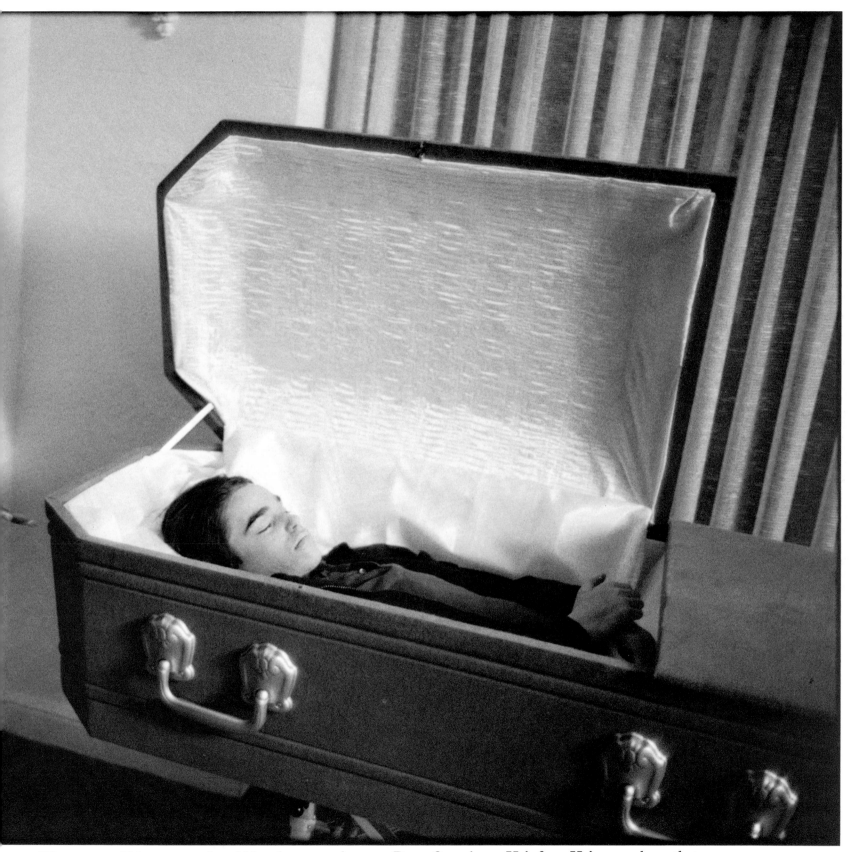

"Dewayne will be cremated and his ashes spread out on Puget Sound . . . He's free. He's never been that way before." JERRY ESTERLY

STREETWISE

What follows is an edited version of the sound track
to the film *Streetwise*. Some material was
omitted because it was repetitious or because,
without the picture, it was unclear. Brief
descriptions of the location and sometimes the
circumstances of the dialogue have been added. The
dialogue was rendered as spoken with special uses
of words, irregularities of grammar and
idiosyncratic syntax preserved to convey the
individuality of each speaker.

N.B.

Early morning on Rainbow Bridge, Rat leaps eighty feet into the water.

RAT (*voice over*)
I love to fly. It's just you're alone, there's peace and quiet, nothing around you but clear blue sky. No one to hassle you. No one to tell you where to go or what to do. The only bad part about flying is having to come back down to the fuckin' world.

Afternoon on Pike Street, Dewayne and Rat panhandle the crowd.

DEWAYNE Spare some change, ma'am, so me and my father could get something to eat?

WOMAN No, I don't, son.

DEWAYNE Alright. (*To Buddha.*) Why not say you're my father?

BUDDHA No. I'm not hungry.

DEWAYNE Alright. Then get lost. I gotta make some money.

DEWAYNE (*voice over*)
Living downtown, a typical day was . . . I'd get up at twelve, take a shower, get something to eat. Three o'clock I was on my robbin' streak, start robbin' people 'til six, seven o'clock. Then I'd go get my drugs, get my food, get my . . . whoever I was going to sleep with that night. Party until twelve. Then everybody would turn in and stuff.

DEWAYNE So what's up?

CHRISSIE Not much.

DEWAYNE Spare some change?

CHRISSIE Hell no.

DEWAYNE How 'bout a kiss?

CHRISSIE Hell no.

DEWAYNE Oh well. Life's hard.

RAT Sir, you wouldn't be able to help me out with a little change, would you?

MAN *NO.*

RAT Not at all, huh. Ya know, you're a fuckin' dick.

RAT (*voice over*)
I wasn't even thinking about running away or nothin'. But my dad told me that if I ever got caught selling pot, never come home 'cause he'd kill me. So when it all came down, I just said, 'oh, well.'

DEWAYNE (*voice over*)
I never miss my mom and dad. They're part of my past now, the way I look at it.

DEWAYNE Where you be livin' at?

RAT (*singing*). I be living at the YMCA . . .

An old abandoned hotel. The windows and doors are boarded up. Inside, Rat roller skates through the empty corridors.

RAT (*voice over*)
There's this old abandoned hotel and we took all the furniture we could find in all the different rooms and put it into this one room. And we'd carry water up in these gallon jugs, 'cause it didn't have no water or electricity. And we'd just shower down at this place called The Compass on Washington Avenue for fifty cents. And do our laundry in the laundromat and whatever it took. It was pretty easy actually.

Rat and his friend Jack in the railroad yard.

RAT (*voice over*)
And then me and Jack just started hanging out together. We're real good friends. He'll treat you right. He won't rip you off. When your back is turned, he ain't gonna stab you. I would never even have thought about catching a train if it weren't for Jack. He showed me the ways of the trains, how they run, where they go. And Jack taught us you can tell the main track 'cause they got a gravel mound and it sets higher than all the other tracks. And then you just look north and that's the north yard. Then you just count three tracks over to your right. And then we'd just jump on a train and be on our way.

Tiny on Pike Street.

TINY (*voice over*)
I wanna be really rich . . . and live on a farm with a bunch of horses, which is my main best animal . . . and have three yachts or more . . . and diamonds and jewels and all that stuff.

Tiny goes to the Adolescent Free Clinic for a gynecological examination.

MEDICAL COUNSELOR So you don't have any symptoms right now, but you do have some concern that you might have a sexually transmitted disease?

TINY Nothing serious. It just might be trichomonas again.

MEDICAL COUNSELOR Did you ever have one before?

TINY Yes.

MEDICAL COUNSELOR What did you have?

TINY I've had chlamydia, trichomonas and gonorrhea.

TINY (*voice over*)
I think it is *very* strange that older men like little girls. They're perverts is what they is. I like the money, but I don't like them.

MEDICAL COUNSELOR You've been sexually active since the time that you were treated?

TINY What do you mean by that?

MEDICAL COUNSELOR Oh, good question. Have you had sex with anyone since you were treated in Portland?

TINY No. Just dates. The first date I turned was about two Thursdays ago. Then I turned another one on Friday.

TINY (*voice over*)
Some dates are nice. And some of them, the young ones are really cute, but I don't want to be interested in them, 'cept for the money, that's it. I used to least bring in $300 or $400. For a blow-job it would be $30 on up and for a lay it would be $40 on up. Most of these veterinarian 'hos would charge more than us little kids do.

TINY Isn't it after every two weeks you can get pregnant, after your period, every two weeks?

MEDICAL COUNSELOR You can get pregnant any time during your cycle. A person can even get pregnant when she's having her period. It's not as likely.

TINY I pulled a date and didn't use a rubber, because he said he didn't use them.

MEDICAL COUNSELOR How often do you usually have your periods?

TINY Every three or four weeks.

MEDICAL COUNSELOR And they come pretty regular?

TINY Well, I just started in August.

MEDICAL COUNSELOR So you'd only had the one in August?

TINY And the one in September.

MEDICAL COUNSELOR So you've barely begun. Did you ever have periods before then?

TINY No.

MEDICAL COUNSELOR You're how old?

TINY Fourteen.

MEDICAL COUNSELOR And how would you feel about being pregnant?

TINY I want a baby. But not by a new trick though.

MEDICAL COUNSELOR What's your feeling about being pregnant now, if the trick is the father?

TINY Well, I'm not getting an abortion.

MEDICAL COUNSELOR You might . . .

TINY No, I would not. I don't believe in them.

MEDICAL COUNSELOR Tell me about that. What's your feeling about abortion?

TINY It's like you're murdering somebody. Murd . . . I can't pronounce the word. But, it's like there's a little baby inside you and you're just killing it. It's not fair to the baby. I mean it's not the baby's fault.

MEDICAL COUNSELOR So, that would not be a choice for you?

TINY No.

Near Pike Street, Tiny gets into the car of an old man.

TINY (*voice over*)
I used to turn dates lots and lots of times. Just about every day I'd be turning dates day and night, day and night. Then I got busted five times. So, now I don't pull dates I don't know.

Rat and Jack in the abandoned hotel.

RAT (*voice over*)
When we'd get real low on money, I'd take Mike's .45, because I'd sold my .38, and I'd go roll a queer.

RAT (*smoking a joint*) Taste's like Colombian to me.

JACK Ain't that bud that's been going around, is it?

RAT Ah, no way. You've got to buy that stuff in grams. I think it went out.

JACK What did?

RAT Oh, I guess not. You know Alan and that guy he was running around with? He had us walking around Mount Vernon for two days looking for this queer that turned him onto all this procaine. We was gonna live in his house for a day. And then when he went to bed we was gonna tie him up and take all his money he had in his wall safe—all this procaine and all this marijuana stuff he had. We walked around Mount Vernon for two days looking for this guy. I finally told Alan and his friend, man, I told him 'fuck off, man.' Me and Mike got on the freeway and hitchhiked all the way up to Bellingham.

JACK That's when you had all of them fuckin' keys and the cops were asking you where you got them. Whatever happened to that Burlington Northern key?

RAT My mom's got all my keys.

Tiny and Kim talk on Pike Street.

KIM My mom, before they went on vacation about four o'clock Friday, she wakes me up and she goes 'We're leaving now.' And I go 'yeah, yeah.' It's four o'clock in the morning. And she goes, 'I know that you're a prostitute and I know what you've been doing and I know that you've got money.' And I jumped up and said, 'Did you look in my purse?' And she goes, 'No.' And I go 'Mom, I am not. Just leave.' And she goes 'Fine. Thanks alot. All week long I'm going to remember this. All week I'm going to be thinking about how much you love me.' I don't care. She doesn't care about me. She never did. She doesn't. Oh well.

TINY My mom cares about me a lot.

KIM Where is she? Where does she live?

TINY She went to Eastern Washington, I think, for the weekend.

KIM That isn't even my real mom. I was adopted. I don't even know who my real parents are. I don't know if they're dead or alive. I'm going to find out though. When I'm eighteen I'm going through the courts to find out. I don't know. Sometimes it seems like a waste of time. If they didn't care enough to keep me, why should I care enough to find out who they are?

TINY Well, they could be rich right now. You know what I'm saying, really rich. Or they could be bums.

Tiny on the street looking for a date.

TINY (voice over)
My real dad I've never known. He could be the guy that's really rich, driving a Mercedes. Or he could be one of these bums on the street. I don't know. I really want to meet him. He could be one of these dates rolling around. I could have dated him for all I know.

Dewayne and Rat talk in an alley off Pike Street.

RAT And your mom is where?

DEWAYNE I don't know, San Diego somewhere. And my dad's in jail.

RAT That sucks.

DEWAYNE Life's a bitch, ain't it?

RAT Are you originally from Seattle?

DEWAYNE Nope. Port Orchard. Well, Washington, yeah. Been in New York once. I hitchhiked there—was there for an hour and left.

RAT What jail's your dad in?

DEWAYNE King County, going up to Walla Walla State Penitentiary for burglary and attempted arson. So where you been living, before you lived in that . . . wherever you live at?

RAT In that hotel?

DEWAYNE Yeah. Is it seriously deserted? How long you been living there?

RAT Shit, since a month after I got to Seattle.

DEWAYNE Where're you from originally?

RAT California.

DEWAYNE What part?

RAT Sacramento.

DEWAYNE I went through there one time. It was bunk.

RAT I don't like Sacramento. I lived right on the outside of Sacramento.

DEWAYNE I went through there and some faggot was tryin' to pick me up, but I robbed him of $150.

RAT Take his car too?

DEWAYNE Hell no. I hitchhike. I love hitchhikin'. Not in Seattle though, 'cause the only ones that'll pick you up are hippies, stoners or fine girls. I like the fine girls to pick me up. (They laugh.)

On Pike Street, Kim and Tiny talk.

KIM I just started doing this stuff. I never even thought of 'hoing 'til I got down here. You know Tracy? She used to live with me when she was a home girl, because her parents kicked her out. And she disappeared. She went downtown with Lorna. You know Lorna? And then Lorna came back and said that Tracy's a 'ho now. And then I got really worried about her. I said, 'I can't let her do that stuff.' 'Cause I always heard bad things like white slavery, that she's gonna get beat up and everything. That's what scared me. So I thought, I gotta come down and get her out of there, whether I gotta kidnap her or what. Then I come down here and I see her and she says, 'It's great, man.' So I'm just sittin' there going 'What? I heard that you don't like it down here, that you're getting beat up and raped and everything.' She said, 'I'm making so much money and it's so easy, the money comes so easy. It's great. You gottta do it.' And I sat there and I go, 'How much money do you make?' and she started naming off and I go, 'Wow! I think I'd better.'

Kim at a pay telephone on Pike Street.

KIM Hi, Sam. This is Kimberly again. So have you decided? Do you want a date tonight?

Pimps on Pike Street; fragments of a conversation.

PATRICE Juan always be lettin' those broads wear his coats and shit. That bitch ain't gonna listen to him for long. She only break $30 wops.

A PIMP Floyd hit me so goddamn hard, when I woke up, man, it was dark. I had to ask people around me what had happened.

PATRICE What're you talking about? I don't do nothin' for free. I'm a pimp. I'm goin' out to those high schools and get me some fresh ones.

In a parking lot near Pike Street, Kim talks to Tiny, Erica, and Kevin about choosing a pimp.

KIM He said, 'If anybody comes to beat you up and I come and save you, that means you gotta work for me.' I hope he doesn't get somebody to come beat me up.

KEVIN No, he isn't. I'll tell you the truth and this is the honest truth. With me, you'll be safer, happier and richer.

ERICA He'll kill you, OK? He'll ass-fuck you, fuck you in the ear or anything. I'm serious, don't mess with Patrice.

KEVIN I don't know about all that, but I know you're making a serious mistake.

TINY Did Patrice try to do anything with you last night?

KIM No.

ERICA He shoots up. He's a drug fiend.

TINY Well, what do you want to do? Who do you want to be with?

KIM I don't know. I'm confused. I don't know who's the right person. I just don't know.

TINY He raped me last year, when I first came downtown . . .

ERICA He raped me too. And he took my *money*. Up in that hotel, he came and said he was gonna rob this dude . . .

TINY He took a fucking coat-hanger and heated it up on the gas heater and said he was gonna beat me if I didn't take off my clothes. I said, 'I ain't takin' off my clothes.'

ERICA We're scaring her.

TINY We don't mean to scare you. We're just telling you the truth. You get beat up and some of these girls end up gettin' killed.

Tiny and Erica leave. Kim and Kevin continue to talk.

KEVIN People get killed down here, they go to jail down here. Everything happens down here and none of it's good.

KIM I haven't seen nobody get killed.

KEVIN I saw a guy get the shit kicked out of him by three niggers over in front of T.J.'s just this morning and get hauled off in the ambulance. He got the shit kicked out of him because he pulled a big ole steak knife out on 'em. You missed that one, dear, but that was just this morning.

KIM So who cares. I don't really care. Whatever happens, happens.

Late afternoon on Pike Street, Chrissie taunts Lillie.

CHRISSIE I should pass the word around. You're a snitch.

LILLIE Chris, just leave me alone.

CHRISSIE Whacha gonna do about it? Huh? Tramp!

LILLIE I'm gonna quit. Sorry, but I ain't a tramp and I ain't a fucking snitch either.

CHRISSIE Come here and say it to my face, you little tramp.

In a parking lot near Pike Street at night.

LULU I want to call your man and tell your man I want to beat you up, but I want to talk to him first, to let him know what's goin' on. 'Cause he's streetwise like a mother-fucker. If you wanna be downtown, you gotta be cool. You better learn the ways of the streets before you start hangin' down here and doin' shit like you're doin'.

BLOND I didn't know I was doin' anything.

Pike Street, at night. Patrice gets arrested. A group of born-again Christians sing hymns. Three boys and a girl have a fist fight in the street, stopping traffic.

Morning comes to an alley lined with garbage dumpsters.

RAT Shit, what is all this shit?

JACK I dunno, come on.

RAT Wanna jacket, a leather jacket?

JACK It's full of grape jelly, man.

Rat and Jack come upon a familiar dumpster and start digging in.

RAT and JACK (*in unison*) It's the Chinese Dumpster!

RAT (*voice over*)
When you get regular dumpsters, we call 'em *regs*, you go there every night. You check all these dumpsters all these different places. And you can tell because they're *regs* what's been there since last week and what was put in there that night. 'Cause alot of people say, 'Shit, that shit could be a week old and you can't even tell,' but you *can* because it's your *reg*, your regular dumpster.

Rat samples some fried chicken.

RAT I think I hit the jackpot.

On Pike Street. Lulu tries to persuade Lillie and her boyfriend to leave.

LULU I told her I'd even get her bus fare, really. I don't want to see her get beat up, she's too young.

LILLIE I'm fifteen.

LULU You ain't *even fifteen*. Don't give me that.

LILLIE By next year I'll be . . .

LULU Bullshit. You're talking shit. How come you can't say it to my face. You ain't fifteen. (*To Lillie's boyfriend.*) She's gonna get you in trouble. Thirteen'll get you twenty.

LULU (*voice over*)
I help a lot of people out. I've talked kids into going home. I ain't got to prove myself to show that I'm a girl. I've thought about not being a lesbian, but then every guy I've ever been with has screwed me over anyway. I get along with straight people too. Just, most of them think that because I'm gay that I'm trying to pick up on their girlfriends. To tell you the truth, I got to like somebody alot to even kiss 'em. See, I'm my own type of person, I am. I protect alot of people. This bum was trying to feel on this friend of mine's chest. I literally walked up and made him come back and apologize to the girl. (*Lulu forces the bum to his knees and slaps him across his face.*) Because she's not public property. I could understand if it was a telephone pole or something, he could touch it then. It's just the way I am. I've been like that since I've been down here. 'Cause nobody did nothin' for me. So, I made him come back and apologize and sent him on his way. I just told him, 'Go on, man, get out of here.' He left. (*Lulu pushes him into the traffic.*)

Tiny visits her mother Pat who works as a waitress at the Coffee Hut.

PAT (*voice over*)
She has grown up quite a bit since she's been on these streets. She's fourteen going on twenty-one.

TINY Extra pickles too, mom, please.

PAT (*to the cook*) Put extra pickles on that.

PAT (*voice over*)
Oh, when I was drinkin', Erin and I used to get in some bad arguments. I could see it in her mind, she's thinkin', 'Oh no, not again.'

TINY (*getting the hamburger*) Mmmmmm. Thank you, mom.

PAT (*voice over*)
I don't know why I started drinkin'. Just cause of boredom half the time. I don't know.

TINY (*shouting to the cook*) Too much *juice.*

PAT Come on, two more bites.

TINY One more. I don't like the bread.

PAT (*voice over*)
See, I've had Erin all my life. I've had to bring her up myself. And then one day I suddenly get married. I think she likes Tom. She just doesn't want to admit it.

TINY (*holding her full stomach*) I feel like I'm pregnant.

PAT (*yawning*) Oh, goodness. (*She serves Tiny some pie.*)

TINY (*sniffing the pie suspiciously*) Don't you have no whipping cream?

PAT No.

PAT (*voice over*)
My fear is that some day I'm going to get a phone call or a knock at my door . . . and she's not going to be there any more.

Tiny and Pat walk to their bungalow.

TINY (*voice over*)
We started living at Larry's a couple of months ago, because my mom and my dad got kicked out of their apartment. And Larry offered them a place to stay. Naturally you call somebody who marries your mother a 'dad.' Sometimes he's an asshole. But he's in the (alcoholic) treatment center. He's going to stay there for two months.

Tiny climbs in the window to open the door from the inside.

PAT Oh, for cryin' out loud. Damn dog. (*Dog yelps.*)

TINY Quit pissin' on the floor now. Look at this mess.

PAT Damn that dog.

TINY You should have left her out . . . What happened to this house? I cleaned it. I'm going to spray some deodorant around here, some Right Guard.

PAT Right Guard? Well, you wanted a dog, Erin, I didn't want her.

They sit down at the kitchen table. Pat does a crossword puzzle and drinks a beer. Tiny goes through the Avon cosmetic book:

TINY I need more make-up, Mom. I want "Cloudy Blue" and "Meadow Violets" and . . .

PAT (*voice over*)
She's always wantin' this and wantin' that. When you're a waitress you just don't make that much. One day she came home and told me she'd made $200. I 'bout fell off my chair.

TINY . . . then I want these three frosts, the blue, the lavender, and "The Best of Bronze."

PAT That costs too much. Look at the price on that!

TINY *Two* for $4.99.

PAT Oh, two.

Tiny moves to the bedroom and their conversation continues from separate rooms.

PAT (*voice over*)
When Erin first told me about this, she thought I would be really angry with her and hate her, but I don't. It's just a phase

she's going through right now. I can't stop her from doing this. She's just going to do it anyway.

TINY Do you think I'd be gettin' that make-up by the end of this month?

PAT Probably about the seventeenth.

TINY Isn't that the day you got married?

PAT Oh, yeah. How 'bout that?

TINY I betcha Dad's goin' start bitchin' at ya.

PAT No. 'Bout what?

TINY Probably wondering if you was sleeping with Larry or not.

PAT Oh, Erin. For heaven's sake.

TINY I'm not saying you did. But that's what he's gonna start bitchin' at you about.

TINY (voice over)
He beats up on my mom. He broke her leg once. He doesn't work. He depends on my mom alot, which is not right. I think the man should support the woman. He says, 'She doesn't have any money.' And I say, 'It's because of *you*. You spend her money on beer. So she doesn't have time for me.' Now my mom's in a mess she can't get out of. I feel really sorry for her.

TINY It'll be a year since you were married. A year has gone by fast, hasn't it? Huh? Mom?

PAT Yes. Don't bug me . . . I'm drinkin'.

Rat does his laundry in a laundromat.

RAT (voice over)
When I first ran away and came here to Seattle, I was tired of being the middleman between my mom and my dad's divorce. I told my mom when I called her about two weeks after I got here that I was in trouble with the law. She understood it. She said, 'Alright, I'll see you when you're eighteen.' And I said, 'Alright.' And then about a month later I called her again and I said, 'Hey mom, how's it goin?' And she said, 'It's awful. I'm broke. He's trying to drain me, trying to make my life miserable.' And she started crying alot, asking me to come home. And I just said, 'Mom, I gotta go' and I hung up on her.

Rat goes outside to panhandle.

RAT Excuse me, sir. Could you spare a dime, so I could finish drying my laundry?

MAN Here you go, son.

RAT Thank you, sir. You have a nice day.

RAT (voice over)
And then I never called her again. I never wrote her a letter or nothin'. Fuck it, ya know. Let her think what she wants, that I'm dead, whatever she wants to think. But I don't want to listen to her cry . . . makin' *me* feel bad.

Reverend Tom Robinson of the Emerald City Mission solicits money on Pike Street. His group sings "If You Want Joy You Must Jump For It."

REVEREND TOM (shouting) That building at 1420 Second Avenue, by the grace of God, will be the new shelter that will sleep two hundred men and fifteen women and two families. And all we asked from you is one dollar. We don't ask for tens, twenties and hundreds, but you let God move on you and you give one dollar and God will bless you. For fourteen years I believed that God was dead. But I do not believe that anymore. Billy Graham convicted me when he pointed his finger right at me and said, *GOD* wants *YOU* to serve *HIM!*

A crowd of street kids gather.

PATRICE When you leave here whachu gonna do? You gonna go home. Right, brother?

REVEREND TOM Sure I am.

PATRICE Yeah, you're gonna go home. And you're gonna go into your *big* house, and get into your *big* bed and sleep with your *big* wife, and all that there, brother.

REVEREND TOM I'm gonna go home and pack food for tomorrow's food bank.

PATRICE OK. What religion are you?

REVEREND TOM I'm Pentecostal. Full Gospel.

PATRICE That's what I was raised as, a Pentecostal. But I don't believe that shit. (To the crowd.) You want to know how they're working us? Remember how when you was in school, once a year they'd tell you to bring your canned goods and give 'em to us? That's what they're doing. They say bring your canned goods and give 'em to us. Then they turn around and give them back to you. (Laughter.) And then they say 'We're doin' something for ya' all.' That's how they're workin' us. I could stand out here and say, 'Yes, Lord. Thank you, Jesus. Gimme a dollar.' I could do that.

REVEREND TOM You could.

PATRICE Yeah, I could. And probably get a dollar.

REVEREND TOM It's your privilege.

PATRICE See, all this is nothin'.

REVEREND TOM But I'm not standing here for me. See, you would be standing here for you.

PATRICE Who are you standing there for?

REVEREND TOM I'm standing here for *you*.

PATRICE You're standing here for *me?* Ain't that nothin'!

REVEREND TOM 'Cause you might be hungry this winter.

PATRICE We're wise out here. We're streetwise. You know that? Everybody's scammin'. You're scammin'. I'm scammin'.

REVEREND TOM Well, you and I'll have to sit down and talk about this. Maybe you can wise me up.

PATRICE Yeah, 'cause you need alot of wisin' if you think you're gonna get rich standing out here. What gives you the audacity to think that we're gonna come off our street life and into your program?

REVEREND TOM I don't wancha in my program.

PATRICE Ah, just a second ago you said . . .

REVEREND TOM All I want to do is give you a good night's sleep.

PATRICE And then I can wake up in the morning, go downstairs and eat some Cabin Crunch . . .

REVEREND TOM Cookies and coffee or whatever we got.

PATRICE Can I bring my girlfriend there if I want to?

REVEREND TOM *Nooo.* If you do, she'll have to stay in a different place.

PATRICE No, brother. It don't work like that.

REVEREND TOM Yeah, it works that way. But I like you, brother.

PATRICE I like you, too. (*They shake hands.*) What's your name? Let me have a card?

REVEREND TOM Tom Robinson. Here's a card.

Rat and Jack scam for dinner.

RAT (*voice over*)
There's many different scams. There's 'Eat and Run.' That's where you go into a restaurant. You order something. Usually they'll set you right by the cash register if you look young and like you don't have any money so they can see you. But right by the cash register is right by the door, so that works out even better. There's also 'Dumpster Diving.' You call Shakeys' Pizza. You can do it right out in front of the restaurant. They got a pay phone right outside. (*Rat enters phone booth.*) You call and order these Hawaiian style pizzas with Canadian bacon and pineapple. They ask your name and your number. You hang up. They call you right back. You say, 'Yeah, I ordered this and this' and they say 'Alright' and you hang up. And then in about an hour, nobody comes to claim the pizza and they set 'em out in the dumpster in the boxes. You go over there and you got six or seven free pizzas. It's easy to survive without pulling tricks or dates on the street.

Patrice shows his own scam to the guys on Pike Street.

PATRICE There it is. (*He opens the bottom of a pack of cigarettes.*) Blotter acid. You get two hits out of every pack, man. Five dol-

lars a hit. It sells like pancakes. Me and Junior made a hundred bucks selling nothing but bunk at a concert. Then we went and bought some good cocaine and *psshhook.* (*Laughing.*)

James goes to a blood bank.

RAT (*voice over*)
You gotta be over eighteen to sell blood, so most of the kids on the street can't sell it, so they can't make money that way. But, if you get a fake ID and you look eighteen, then you can go there and sell blood.

NURSE (*to James*) The first one you do, the last two we do. But you make sure that we do them. It's your responsibility to make sure that you walk out of here alive . . . OK, make a fist for me.

In the corner of Second and Pike Streets, William takes Lulu on. A crowd gathers.

WILLIAM If you're a goddamn woman, Lulu, why don't you act like one?

LULU Fuck you. I don't have to act like all these bitches down here.

WILLIAM I'm not talking about acting like a bitch. I'm talking about acting like a woman, Lulu. You don't do that.

LULU You ain't my man. You don't tell me shit.

WILLIAM I wouldn't be your man even if you liked men.

LULU You can't tell me shit.

WILLIAM Bitch, I'm tellin' you all kinds of things.

LULU Fuck you, punk.

WILLIAM Bitch.

LULU Punk.

WILLIAM 'Ho.

LULU Punk.

WILLIAM Tramp.

LULU What about your K.C.? The one with the burning goddamn gonorrhea.

LULU (*voice over*)
I ain't putting on a dress for nobody. I haven't done it since I was sixteen. I've had my nose broke five times. I've had both sets of my eye bones broke, top and bottom. I've had my jaw cracked three times. I'll tell people now, they can beat the shit out of me, but they're not getting me away from down here.

On Pike Street, Dewayne comes on to Kim.

KIM Calvin and Erica been down here?

DEWAYNE Erica was.

KIM This girl told me they're after my ass. I gotta keep it cool.

DEWAYNE Man, I wouldn't even worry about them.

KIM There are alot of people after my ass 'cause I'm not working any more.

DEWAYNE Well, be with me and you wouldn't have to work.

KIM (*laughing*) Naw.

DEWAYNE I'm serious. No mother-fucker's gonna fuck with you.

KIM I'm just not going to come down here any more.

DEWAYNE Then let me get your phone number, so I can call you, so we can go out for pizza or somethin'.

KIM I don't have a phone right now.

DEWAYNE Well, let me give you my number and you can call me.

KIM OK, whatever.

DEWAYNE Anybody got a pen? I don't got no pen. There's a pen, thank you sir. Now, anybody got a piece of paper?

Dewayne goes to the Adolescent Free Clinic to find out why he is so small for his age.

DR. DEISHER Well, you gained about 3 inches in height, since we last saw you almost a year and a half ago. You haven't gained much weight. You're about the same weight as you were.

DEWAYNE I eat all the time, but I don't gain no weight or nothin'. I think there's a worm inside me or somethin'.

DR. DEISHER Think you got worms, huh?

DEWAYNE I dunno. I want to get it checked out.

DR. DEISHER Sure. Can you straighten up? (*Dewayne uncurls his spine from its usual slouch.*) Do you spend alot of time on the streets?

DEWAYNE Yup.

DR. DEISHER What do you do down there?

DEWAYNE Panhandle. Just hang around. Hug all the girls.

DR. DEISHER You got alot of girlfriends?

DEWAYNE Yup.

DR. DEISHER Hummmm. Let's see those tonsils. (*He slips a tongue depresser into Dewayne's mouth.*)

DEWAYNE Awgh.

DR. DEISHER Take it easy. When did you have tonsillitis last?

DEWAYNE Awwgh. When I was locked up in Echo Glen, that was maybe two months ago.

DR. DEISHER Did you go to school last year?

DEWAYNE Nope. For two years I haven't been to school.

DR. DEISHER So you haven't been to school since you were twelve?

DEWAYNE No. I'm sixteen.

DR. DEISHER (*feeling the glands in Dewayne's neck*) Does it hurt when I do this?

DEWAYNE Nope. It feels good.

DR. DEISHER What do you think you'd like to do someday?

DEWAYNE I dunno.

DR. DEISHER Anything interest you at all?

DEWAYNE Nope.

DR. DEISHER You got lots of big glands in your neck. You got chronically infected tonsils, which certainly don't help your growth and your nutrition any.

DEWAYNE I might join the Navy, if the world lasts that long. Reagan's sending all them Marines, shootin' everybody. All them Marines get to shootin', cuttin' out Russia and Russia's probably gonna bomb us or somethin'. Ow, that hurts right there.

DR. DEISHER That hurts, huh? Does it hurt bad or just a little?

DEWAYNE Just a little. Ow, right there. Oh, yeah.

Rat, Jack, and Shadow look at knives in a pawn shop window.

RAT You mean you ain't got fifty cents? Why don't you just walk up to some guy and ask him for fifty cents to catch the bus?

SHADOW 'Cause I don't have a face like yours.

RAT Aw, it'll work.

Shadow leaves.

RAT (*to Jack*) He's the worst one on Pike Street. He'll be your buddy when you're face to face. As soon as you turn around, you got a knife in your back. It ain't worth it.

Shadow sits alone on Pike Street.

SHADOW (*voice over*)
You learn how to fight, one way or another. Or you disappear. I know how to fight, but I like disappearing. My mother and father got a divorce when I was about a year old. My mother decided I should go to a foster home. About five years ago, my father said, 'I want you to come over.' So, I spent six months with my father. Six months were up, nobody could find my mother. A year went up, nobody could find my mother. My father got tired of me and my sister. He told me to leave. I left.

Shellie uses a pay telephone on Pike Street to phone home.

SHELLIE Hi. Is mom there? Howya doin'? . . . Nothing, just called to tell you I'm OK and shit . . . Where am I? None of your business . . . No. Call me a prostitute. Come on, I dare you to . . . No, that's not what I'm doing but that's what you called me last time I was gone . . . Yes you did . . . I called to tell you I'm OK, to see how you were doin' and now I'm going to hang up . . . and I hope you have fun with your stupid-ass husband. (*To Shadow.*) Ooooo, she pisses me off.

Shadow and Shellie go the amusement park together.

SHADOW (*voice over*)
Shellie's a real sweet girl. The streets is nothing for a girl that young. I mean, fourteen years old and on the streets . . . I've taken care of her a little, made sure she's eaten. She's like a little sister . . . I like women for the simple reason they're sweet, they're caring, they need care.

SHELLIE One thing I don't do is fall in love in two or three days. I've made many mistakes . . .

SHADOW You've never lived on the streets.

SHELLIE I have so lived on the streets before.

SHADOW Not like this. Not like I have.

SHELLIE I don't want to live on the streets like you have. I'm not going to either, man.

SHADOW Are you going to help me dye my hair?

SHELLIE Hell, no. I can't dye hair, man.

SHADOW I'll do it myself then. I don't know how I'm going to do it, but I'm going to do it myself.

SHELLIE Why do you want your hair dyed? To change?

SHADOW Not actually to change, to get away from everything.

SHELLIE That ain't gonna get you away from jack-shit, honey.

SHADOW It will, considering I'm gonna dye my hair.

SHELLIE (*voice over*)
My mom's got seven kids. She's thirty-two. My wishes would be to have a small family that was happy. Just my older brother, my real dad and me and my mom. Nobody else.

Shellie at home with her mother.

SHELLIE'S MOTHER I can't have you livin' out on the streets.

SHELLIE So, I can't have me living here.

MOTHER I'm trying to get some input from you Shellie. Anything but sarcasm.

SHELLIE That's all I get around here. That's all I ever hear from Larry.

MOTHER That's his way of dealing with people.

SHELLIE Right. He makes me sick . . . from when I was little and he was a pervert and shit. Every time I remember what he did to me, when he took advantage of me and shit.

MOTHER I didn't know and you didn't tell me.

SHELLIE *I DIDN'T KNOW IT.* Until you started asking me.

MOTHER But you wouldn't tell me then.

SHELLIE When you asked me if he did a certain thing, I said, 'yeah.' And then you went and told him. Ever since then he's hated me.

MOTHER Yeah, but he didn't do it any more.

SHELLIE So. I still hate him for doing it to begin with.

Shellie sitting on a bench on Pike Street eating a pizza with Patti and Munchkin.

SHELLIE (*voice over*)
Shadow asked me if he found a place for me to stay, a permanent place, would I stay there. I said, 'Yeah, probably.' He said, 'Well, Patti and Munchkin say you can stay with them.' They needed the money for rent.

SHADOW (*voice over*)
I grew up with Munchkin. For a long time I ran around with him. And Patti, I met her down here about three years ago beatin' the heck out of some old dude 'cause he said somethin' wrong to her.

Patti and Munchkin kissing on Pike Street.

SHADOW (*voice over*)
Patti and Munchkin are very . . . they were, in my eyes, made for each other. They argue, but doesn't all love affairs argue? Patti and Munchkin are a team. That's the way they work the best. A street couple that are struggling to survive.

Rat and Jack shower at the Lutheran Compass Center.

RAT (*voice over*)
Every person, no matter how big or tough they are, should always have a partner. You never want to go on the streets alone. It's a mistake. It's just you'll get lonely, you'll get upset, you'll get beat up. Because, you never can tell if someone's gonna come up from the front of you and start to get your attention, and this other dude is gonna walk up behind you and bust your fuckin' head. Partners are always better.

Shadow takes a motel room for the night to dye his hair. He kneels on the bathroom floor reading the instructions on the package.

SHADOW Mix all mixture and thoroughly saturate hair. Loosely pile hair on top of head. Leaves your hair silky, shiny, and free of tangles.

Looking at himself in the mirror, Shadow massages the dye into his hair.

SHADOW (*voice over*)
I consider myself a playboy. As a boyfriend, you're obligated to one girl. I considered myself dependent upon a couple of girls supporting me. But as far as being a pimp, I never pushed them out onto the streets. You can't be a boyfriend and have three girlfriends. But you can be a playboy. A playboy is what I consider myself.

Tiny and Shellie in a video arcade.

SHELLIE Now she's married again. That's why I'm not at home. 'Cause I can't stand my step-dad.

TINY Nobody can stand their step-dads.

SHELLIE Some people get along fine with them. My first step-dad was OK.

Dewayne visits his father in prison. Lee is behind a glass partition. They speak using telephones.

LEE I got an idea that's fantastic. We'll make some money and we'll put it in 'Lee & Sons Thrift Shop.' We're gonna open up our own store, like that thrift store I had. When I get out, as soon as I'm out a little while, I want you to come with me 'cause I've already talked to some people about a building in maybe Redland. Look around out there. See if there's any good thrift shops out there.

DEWAYNE Alright.

LEE I was supposed to get out this Friday, but I won't because I've got to wait for the damn parole board. If it'd just been that burglary it'd be alright, but it was that stupid arson thing. So the board wants to talk to me. And like everybody says, I've done thirty years—what the hell good is it going to do to make me do a couple more years. I've only got three years left on my 'max.'

DEWAYNE Are you in a cell by yourself.

LEE No, I'm in the 'mean tank.' That's for guys who've done time and everything before.

DEWAYNE For a felony and stuff?

LEE Yeah.

DEWAYNE Is a bunch of The Jokers in there?

LEE Two of 'em are, yeah.

DEWAYNE Is one Stubbs?

LEE Yeah.

DEWAYNE Tell him I said 'hi.'

LEE Yeah, yeah. What's this? You're gonna have to take your tonsils out?

DEWAYNE They say it's always infected and stuff, so I don't know. They think that's why I'm so small and stuff.

LEE You know that's funny. I was that way, too.

DEWAYNE Were you small like this?

LEE Yeah. They took them out and about a year after that I got almost as big as I am now.

DEWAYNE I eat all the time but I don't gain no weight. So you think it's just . . . whadaya call it?

LEE Tonsils and adenoids.

DEWAYNE Yeah, but . . .

LEE Hed . . . heditary . . . hereditary.

DEWAYNE Yeah.

LEE How much are you smoking?

DEWAYNE I'm cutting down to maybe four cigarettes a day. Four or five.

LEE That's good. (*He lights a cigarette.*) Don't smoke too much 'cause that's bad too. Still messin' with that weed?

DEWAYNE A little.

LEE How 'bout anything else?

DEWAYNE Nope.

LEE Let me see your arms.

DEWAYNE My arms? Why?

LEE Undo your sleeve.

DEWAYNE Naw, I haven't been doing none of that. Here I'll even show you. See. Nothin'.

LEE What are you messin' with?

DEWAYNE Nothin'.

LEE You're a smart kid. You're a good-looking kid. You've got intelligence. You've got my brain. (*Laughs.*) But you're like me. You're a con man, Dewayne. Whadaya wanna be? A little punk on the street? A little smart-ass little punk. That's all you think you are. You're going to wind up just like I am. Look at me when I talk at you. That's the dang trouble, you haven't paid any attention to me. There's a guy in our tank, twenty-four years old. They just gave him four life sentences. Twenty-four years old. It won't be too many damn years they'll be doing that to you. They're not going to slap your little hand and send you off to Echo Glen or some damn place. Is that what you want?

DEWAYNE No.

LEE You say that now 'cause you're sittin' here talking to me. Get your hands out of your mouth! Let me see your fingers. Still biting your damn nails, ain't you? When are you gonna stop doin' that? Huh? You're out there, tough guy on the street. Big-time tough little punk is all you are. Can't even quit biting your fingernails. You're too goddamn little to be tough, kid . . . I'm serious. I love you very, very much, even though I get mad and want to kill you. I love you. You're all I got. And unfortunately, I'm all *you've* got. I'm gonna make it up to you . . . for all the stuff we didn't do. I know I have to talk rough to you some-times, Dewayne, but you know that I love you a whole big, big bunch. If I get out this time, I'll keep you straight and you keep me straight. Is that a deal? Just remember, you and I is all we got. Together ain't nobody can whip us, ain't nobody can do anything to us. I love you.

DEWAYNE Bye-bye.

Dewayne leaves. His father waves goodbye through the glass partition.

Patrice runs into his mother and her friend by accident in a parking lot near Pike Street.

MOTHER Look at you. All beat up and cut up and scarred up and drugged up. I haven't seen you in two months. You didn't even call me. I can't get over that. After I sent for you all the way from California, down there stranded. And you didn't even thank me. You ought to thank me now.

PATRICE Thank you, mom. (*They kiss.*)

MOTHER'S FRIEND Call her up. You can call her up. Nikita and them calls me and Todd calls me. Do you love your mother?

PATRICE Yes.

MOTHER When are you gonna show me? When are you gonna make me proud?

MOTHER'S FRIEND So that's what you should do, you should stop and see mom, you know what I mean. 'Cause she is the only one gotta guide map to your life. 'Cause you can't go nowhere unless you ask your mother advices and things, you know that?

MOTHER He don't want no advice right now. He thinks he's doin' it.

MOTHER'S FRIEND That's why he's gettin' knocked around and beat around, too.

MOTHER You think you're doin' it? I love you, Patrice. You wanna go eat somethin'? I'm not gonna just give you my money, now. If you wanna go eat somethin', I'll feed you.

PATRICE I'm not hungry, ma.

MOTHER Yes, ya are.

MOTHER'S FRIEND What did you eat today?

PATRICE Some cookies and ah . . .

MOTHER'S FRIEND Junk food.

PATRICE . . . and some juice.

MOTHER You want something hot in your stomach? That's what you need. If I give you some of my money, whacha gonna do with it?

PATRICE Save it.

MOTHER Oh, yeah. How're you gonna save it out here? You'll just tell me anything just to shut me up.

MOTHER'S FRIEND I'm tellin' ya. He gonna save it. (*Laughing.*)

MOTHER (*to her friend*) You got some money?

MOTHER'S FRIEND Just a little change.

MOTHER If I think you're buying a pack of cigarettes, next time I see you I won't give you a dollar.

PATRICE OK.

MOTHER'S FRIEND Or some weed.

MOTHER You'd better not! You know that's hard-work money. I worked for that money. You spend it wisely, OK? When you get straight, you know where your house is.

PATRICE OK.

MOTHER'S FRIEND And the only way you can really get straight is to stay in touch with mom, because you can't straighten yourself.

Lulu on Pike Street.

LULU (*voice over*)
I have seven brothers and sisters. I lost one seven months ago from cirrhosis of the liver. She was twenty-six. I loved her alot. It made me sort of loony for about a month. People thought I was going crazy. I wasn't going crazy, I just couldn't handle it.

Lulu fights with a cop.

LULU (*shouting*) I just got out of jail not even a month ago. I ain't gettin' in no trouble, punk. I bet you I got a bruise on my arm, guaranteed. And I'm pressing charges on your ass. Punk. 'Cause I hate you and I'm gonna git you for that.

Another cop arrives in a squad car.

SECOND COP What's the trouble here, young man?

LULU I'm not a him. I'm a her. I'm pressing charges . . .

SECOND COP Will you please calm down?

LULU I'm pressing charges on him. I want you to know that right now.

SECOND COP Alright, you do that.

LULU Are you a sergeant?

SECOND COP I'm asking you to please calm down.

LULU I'm calm.

SECOND COP Now will you please leave because we have quite a crowd here?

LULY (*walking off, screaming at the first cop*) YOU'RE A PUNK! PUNK!

Shadow gets a dragon tattooed on his forearm.

SHADOW (*voice over*)
Giving blood, there's pain. Falling in love, there's pain. All you feel is the first initial needle. The rest is lingering pain from when the needle pulled out.

Patti gives Munchkin a permanent.

PATTI Honey, come and help me figure this out. Now hold this. Right here. Bring your head back up here.

MUNCHKIN The shit burns my eyes, I'm telling you.

PATTI Not supposed to have your eyes open.

MUNCHKIN Yeow, you poked me in the eye now.

PATTI Stop being a jerk.

MUNCHKIN Thanks. You just wiped it right across my fuckin' eye. God, man.

PATTI Why doncha do your own fuckin' permanent.

Jerry Esterly, Patti's probation officer, pays a call on Patti and Munchkin at their boarding house.

JERRY (*voice over*)
I probably have about a hundred kids on my case load. 'Course Patti is Patti. She's an individualist. She'll go along with you if you're doin' what she wants, but she ain't gonna do a damn thing she doesn't want to do.

JERRY I knocked on the door and I was just worried about you.

PATTI (*in a towel and shower cap*) I don't care how worried you're gettin' about me. All I gotta say is that you don't got no right walkin' in my house.

JERRY But this morning, we've got job therapy . . .

PATTI We know that, Jerry. But you gotta understand that you can't just be walking into my house. You might get shot as far as you know.

JERRY Well, I took the chance on ya wouldn't shoot me. And then I banged on the door.

PATTI Well, the next time you're gettin' shot, OK?

JERRY OK . . . So the rent's due today, right?

PATTI No . . .

JERRY And if you're gonna stay here . . .

MUNCHKIN Not from what Bob says. I told Bob I'd give him $20 and the rest on Friday.

JERRY This is the deal. If you're gonna stay here, you gotta go out to job therapy.

PATTI You can't tell me what to do.

JERRY Patti, we've been together . . .

PATTI You and me ain't been together.

JERRY We have. We've been working together, Patti. And I'm concerned about you. I don't want you guys to have to hit the bricks again. I don't want you to have to get back into some crap that you shouldn't be involved in to pay your rent. You've got a chance to make it a good way, OK? Now this guy has got some ideas that can help you get a job. That's a better life for you than having to be hustling on the streets or be down there pushing . . .

PATTI Who says we're hustling down on the streets, huh Jerry?

JERRY Oh, come on. How else you gonna make your money?

On Pike Street, kids are hanging out. Girls are looking for dates, including Patti.

RAT (*voice over*)
Most of the kids on the street, that's how they survive. They feel like if they don't do the dates, that they're gonna be broke, they're gonna have to dumpster dive, they're gonna have to beg for money. And that's gonna make them feel, 'cause they're girls, like 'Oh, I'm no good. I'm dirty, I'm rotten, I'm a scum, I'm living in this rat-hole, no water, no electricity, no nothing, I'm beggin' for money.' I guess they feel that's worse than pullin' dates. I don't know what their problem is.

Tiny and Shellie talk in a parking lot near Pike Street.

SHELLIE Munchkin's the one that wants us out there 'hoing and shit, and I don't want to do it. The only reason I'm out there is, like I said, Patti's out there and she has to have somebody with her. And when I moved in with them, I said, 'Patti, I don't wanna be 'hoing or anything.' She said, 'You won't be. Munchkin's not gonna pimp you or nothin.'

TINY Do you turn dates now?

SHELLIE Hell, yeah. Me and Patti do. I try to tell Patti I don't want to and she'll start bitchin' at me saying that I just missed a hundred dollar date. Every time I fuck up she says it was a hundred dollar date.

TINY When you do make money, do you give it to Munchkin?

SHELLIE I give it to Patti and Patti gives it to Munchkin.

TINY And you haven't got nothin' out of it, huh?

SHELLIE Me and Patti are both mad right now, because he's sending both of us out there to get him a suit! All he wants is a whole bunch of clothes and shit. Get this, Patti hasn't pulled any dates today and I did two. Forty bucks each. Well, I told her I can't handle this. I'm gonna take off and shit. Last night she says 'you ain't goin' nowhere.' And I said, 'Yes I am.' This morning she was even talking all this shit about how she was gonna sock me if I even tried to go up there and stuff. I mean I was just trippin' out. How the hell can these people think they own me. Nobody does.

TINY You can end up with the wrong people down here.

SHELLIE You wanna know who set me up with the wrong people?

TINY Who?

SHELLIE A person by the name of Shadow.

Shellie and Shadow talk in a parking lot.

SHADOW You changed too. When I first ran into you, you were real sweet . . .

SHELLIE I still am.

SHADOW Oh, yeah. When you ended up at George's you were a real pain in the ass. Now you're even worse.

SHELLIE I was a real pain in the ass, because you fuckin' bull-shitted me. You don't bull-shit me!

SHADOW But I keep wantin' to. I don't know why. Probably because I like you.

SHELLIE (*laughing, embarrassed*) Drop that cigarette!

SHADOW It's not done . . . Now it's done.

A bum serenades Rat and Tiny on the pier.

BUM (*fortissimo*) America, America. God shed His life on ya'll.

RAT (*voice over*)
I like alot of the girls on the street. Tiny, I like her especially. She's a sweet girl.

RAT Wanna go swimmin'?

TINY Ya think I'm crazy or somethin'? Right, let's just jump in.

RAT Alright . . . How about a back flip?

Rat does a back flip into the water. He swims back towards Tiny.

TINY (*voice over*)
The reason why I think Rat it cute, and the reason why I love

him so much, is because he's got pretty eyes. I think they're brown or blue, one or the other.

Rat and Tiny go to the abandoned hotel. Tiny runs down the corridor and into Rat's room. Rat skates after her.

RAT I gotta go back to school someday. 'Cause I need a diploma, so I can get into the Air Force. But right now it's the Open Road, USA for me.

TINY Check you out!

RAT (*voice over*)
I didn't talk to her much about being a prostitute. She hadn't done it that often from what she told me.

RAT Now where's my kiss, honey-bunch?

TINY Not with braces.

Dewayne, in Juvenile Detention, gets a visit from Jerry Esterly.

DEWAYNE I'm the smallest guy in the unit.

JERRY Yeah, for a while I thought you might be in the other unit.

DEWAYNE Junior boys? Naw, because of my age. So when will I be released?

JERRY OK, here's the deal. I got a phone call from Kim yesterday, and I wasn't in. Then I phoned Kim this morning 'cause I needed to talk to her before you get out of here. So all I can do is just keep trying. And as soon as I get a hold of her, I've given permission for her to come down and get you. Kim, with that new baby, she doesn't need these problems. You're in a really touchy situation anyway. You're living with an 18-year old who used to be real active on the streets herself.

DEWAYNE Kim's twenty.

JERRY Is she twenty now? OK, legally, she's not a foster parent. I think it's really good, you guys are working out like a family. And I think it's a good arrangement for you. But I don't want you getting busted and messing that up. OK?

DEWAYNE Alright.

JERRY Right now you're charged with selling pot. So as far as you staying away from downtown, I don't care if you stay away from downtown or not. You've got a lot of friends down there. I think that you have to use your own judgment on that. OK? You know the things you'd better not be doing downtown. I mean, the police, everybody knows you down there. If you're dealing dope, they're gonna bust you again. And if you get busted again, then you're not going to get out of here until after your hearing.

Rat and Tiny sitting on Rat's bed in the abandoned hotel.

RAT (*voice over*)
She'll start talking about 'Oh, I wanna have a kid' and all this shit. She just wants to get too serious at too young of an age. She's only fourteen years old and she makes it sound like she's ready to get married.

TINY Well, then don't leave.

RAT I got to.

TINY No you don't.

RAT Yeah, I gotta get Mike out of Juvenile Hall.

TINY Why?

RAT Because. I can't have my best friend locked up. I gotta go break him out.

TINY (*Laughs.*) Check you out.

RAT I'm serious. I'm gonna go break him out. Then we're gonna go to Florida.

TINY And what if you get caught?

RAT Well, I'll still be with him. (*Laughs.*) They'll throw me in jail right along with him.

TINY Then take me with you.

RAT Women are a pain in the ass on the road.

Tiny's mother goes to an alcoholic treatment center.

TINY (*voice over*)
We got into a fight. She was drunk that night. She was slappin' on me and I was slappin' back on her, because she hit me and I hit her back. The next day she felt really bad.

PAT (*voice over*)
Finally one day I woke up and said 'I'm an alcoholic.' I'd better do something about it.

TINY Good-bye, mama.

PAT Good-bye, honey. I love you. I'll be back.

On Pike Street at night, Lulu finds a girl crying.

LULU What's your name? Did somebody hurt you? What did they do to you? Really, I won't hurt you. (*To the arriving paramedic.*) Looks like her jaw is broke.

PARAMEDIC Her jaw is broken?

LULU She's been bangin' her head against the wall.

PARAMEDIC (*to the girl*) Look up for a second. We want to look at your eyes.

LULU Her eyes are rolling.

PARAMEDIC Did anybody see what happened? What has she been taking?

LULU I don't know.

PARAMEDIC Open your eyes.

LULU Her tongue was stickin' out.

PARAMEDIC Come on now. Open your eyes. We're here to help you.

LULU I asked her if she wanted me to call a doctor and she said 'Yeah.' I think somebody assaulted her to tell you the truth.

PARAMEDIC Does anybody know her here?

LULU No.

Rat visits Tiny in Juvenile Detention.

MATRON You have a half an hour for visiting. (*She leaves.*)

TINY A half hour.

RAT You're stupid!

TINY I am not. It wasn't my fault.

RAT Well, if you wouldn't have been in that next room hangin' your fuckin' head out the window yelling, 'Hey guys, I'm over here. Look.'

TINY I didn't say that!

RAT Can't ever keep your fucking head in, can you? Like Brian says, you can take the 'ho off the street, but not the street off the 'ho. Oh, well. I guess it doesn't matter to me. I didn't get arrested.

TINY You're lucky. You're really lucky.

RAT You just gotta stay one step ahead.

TINY You left me there!

RAT That's right. I sure did. You didn't say, 'Hey Rat, where're you going? Hey Rat, take me with you.'

TINY I woulda never got caught. I wouldn't be in here 'til Monday.

RAT I'll be gone by Monday.

TINY I don't want you to leave. Why can't you wait 'til next Sunday.

RAT 'Cause, I got places to go and things to do.

TINY Wait 'til next Sunday. Come on. This is the last time you get to see me.

RAT Well, well . . . You missed a good fight. Lulu kicked this one whore's ass. She said, 'You bitch' and she fuckin' smashed her right in the face. She didn't smack her, she punched her. The broad fell down and jumped up and took off running all the way up to Pike Street and then ran . . .

TINY Who was this girl?

RAT She's sort of tall. She's real skinny, like you. And she's got real dark, short hair, black hair. I'd show her to you but you ain't getting out 'til Monday, and I'm leaving Sunday.

TINY Why? Why do you have to leave a day before I get out?

RAT Why? Because Monday, Mike gets out. I'm going to break him out Monday. Thump, take their cuff keys. Open the door, take Mike's cuffs off and off to Alaska we go. It's that simple. Maybe we'll stop through here and pick you up. Doubt it, but maybe. Oh, well, so long . . . Tiny . . . Hey Tiny. What's the matter?

TINY Nothing.

RAT If nothing's the matter, then why're you crying?

TINY You should have figured it out by now.

RAT Well, I gotta go.

TINY Go, then.

RAT Don't I at least get a hug good-bye?

They hug for a long moment and Rat leaves. Tiny sits down on the bed and sobs.

Rat goes down to the pier and watches a ferry come in. A freight train moves off, leaving Seattle. Rat hops on and disappears between the cars.

An empty funeral parlor with a closed casket.

JERRY (*voice over*)
I found out in the morning that there'd been a suicide. I didn't know who it was and I didn't think of Dewayne, even though I knew he was in that institution. Dewayne hung himself. The one thing that Dewayne wanted was a family. And he wanted to grow up as what he saw as just a regular kid. I think he sort of had that dream of a mother and a father and a house in the country, maybe a horse or a bicycle to ride on. He just wanted what every kid has a right to have, I think.

At the funeral home, Dewayne's father, handcuffed to a prison guard, comes in and sits down. Three more people follow.

JERRY (*voice over*)
At the funeral home, there was his father. There were prison guards because of his dad's status. Three other people, all three who worked with Dewayne in one way or another as part of the Social Service Agencies. And that was it. So it was pretty much as his life had been. A pretty lonely, pretty skimpy affair.

MINISTER Lord, in our lives, we are often confused and we often ask '*why?*' But it is times like these when our '*why*' becomes our strongest cry.

Flashback of Dewayne on Pike Street.

DEWAYNE (*voice over*)
Get a girl friend, have a house or a car or somethin'. Have a little money in the bank, get a job. That's what I expect out of life. Not much.

Lee sits handcuffed to a guard beside the coffin.

LEE "I love you. And I'm sorry. But I'll see you."

A small boat moves slowly across Puget Sound in the morning mist.

JERRY (*voice over*)
It's my understanding that Dewayne will be cremated and his ashes spread on Puget Sound. Dewayne was a street kid. Dewayne drifted all his life. And it seemed better for me than just putting him in the ground in a box where's he's got to be there. He's free. He's never been that way before.

Take Care of All of My Children
Words and music by Tom Waits

Take care of all of my children
      Don't let them wander and roam.
Take care of all of my children
      For I don't know when I'm coming back home.

You can put all of my possessions here in Jesus' name
      And nail a sign on the door.
Bright and early Sunday morning with my walking cane,
      I'm going up to see my Lord.

Keep them together at the sundown
      Safe from the devil's hand.
You got to make them a pillow on the hard ground.
      I'll be going up to Beulah land.

You can put all of my possessions here in Jesus' name
      And nail a sign on the door.
Bright and early Sunday morning with my walking cane,
      I'm going up to see my Lord.

Remember you never trust the devil,
      Stay clear of Lucifer's hand.
Don't let them wander in the meadow,
      Or you'll wind up in the frying pan.

You can put all of my possessions here in Jesus' name
      And nail a sign on the door,
Bright and early Sunday morning with my walking cane,
      I'm going up to see my Lord.

Tiny, Halloween, 1983.